Darfield & Wombwell

BRIAN ELLIOTT

Brian Elliott (signature)

SUTTON PUBLISHING

Sutton Publishing Limited
Phoenix Mill · Thrupp · Stroud
Gloucestershire · GL5 2BU

First published 2001

Reprinted in 2001

Title page photograph: Wombwell's heritage is celebrated in this iron archway which faces High Street from Pearsons Field. It was designed by the young people of Wombwell and executed by Lesley Fallais and Les Biggs. A commemorative plaque informs us that the refurbished town centre was officially opened on 18 December 1999 by Mayor Howard Lavender. The project was sponsored by Barnsley Metropolitan District Council, Yorkshire Forward and the European Development Fund.

British Library Cataloguing in Publication Data
A catalogue record for this book is available from the British Library.

ISBN 0-7509-2713-5

Typeset in 10.5/13.5 Photina.
Typesetting and origination by
Sutton Publishing Limited.
Printed and bound in England by
J.H. Haynes & Co. Ltd, Sparkford.

> *For Elaine and David,*
> *Esther and Martyn*

An interesting early view of Church Street, Darfield, *c.* 1905. It had the benefit of a single gas lamp. The gable end of the old tithe barn can be seen in front of All Saints' Church. Across the street the signboard is for the old Cross Keys Inn which stood next to the ivy-clad vicarage. *Margaret Mann*

CONTENTS

The place-name Darfield, or 'Dereweld' as it was anciently written, means 'open land frequented by deer' and in some documents it is given as 'Derfeld-on-Dearne'. But the '-field' element also suggests a treeless area in an otherwise woodland environment. The presence of the local names Upperwood, Middlewood and Netherwood add credence to this and are tantalising reminders of a long-lost landscape. This Edwardian postcard helps us appreciate the hill-top setting chosen by the Anglo-Saxons for the site of their village, which may have had a small timber church, replaced and enlarged in stone by later Norman builders.

Central Wombwell from the air, 1995. Features marked are: A = parish church; B = old town hall; C = public library; D = Churchill Hotel; E = markets; F = Park Street/High Street; and G = Church Street/Hough Lane. *Wes Hobson*/Barnsley Chronicle

INTRODUCTION

The location of the parish of Darfield at the eastern side of the coal measures, less than 5 miles from Barnsley and 9 from Doncaster, meant that it lay on the ancient salters' trade route that linked Cheshire and the western Pennines to eastern England. Since Wombwell was also a stopping place on the old highway that stretched from London towards Richmond and Edinburgh, it is not surprising that a considerable amount of traffic of people and goods passed through the parish. Chapter 2, *Finding the Way*, offers some visual glimpses of the tremendous importance of communications in Darfield and Wombwell's history.

The old and extensive parish of Darfield in Strafforth Wapentake consisted of five townships, namely Darfield, Wombwell, Billingley, Little Houghton and Great Houghton. Anciently, Ardsley and Worsbrough also formed part of the parish but they lay within Staincross Wapentake and have not been included in this book. Tantalising visual evidence of several very interesting medieval sites and settlements within the parish are referred to in Chapter 1, *Knights, Farmers & Innkeepers*.

All Saints' Church at Darfield is one of the most splendid medieval country churches in South Yorkshire, with a continuity of worship that probably stretches back to at least the eleventh century. 'At least' in the sense that there may well have been a pre-Conquest building on or near the site in an area where there is certain evidence of Roman activity. The chance finds of hoards of Roman coins during building work at Darfield in 1947, 1948 and 1950 is unlikely to be the last that we hear about a much earlier landscape.

In 1879, just at the time when large collieries were making a significant mark on the local landscape, the Rector of Darfield described his parish in language worthy of any tourist guide: 'The parish of Darfield is situated in the finest part of the West Riding, celebrated for the salubrity of its air and the excellency of its soil, being amply provided with wood and coal and minerals'. Despite the impact of coal mining, Darfield did retain a great deal of its village character. Activities such as quarrying and the making of grindstones took place within the context of farm work, and alongside traditional crafts and small businesses. Well into the twentieth century you could buy pots and pans, house furnishings and groceries and even have a suit made without having to travel into Barnsley or Doncaster. Billingley and to a lesser extent Great and Little Houghton also functioned as agricultural settlements despite the unmistakable presence of nearby collieries. Family names such as Beevors, Carr, Goldthorpe, Hammerton, Hirst, Lazenby, Middleton, Needham, Roystone and Stables, all listed in nineteenth-century trade directories for Darfield, can still be found in the *The Phone Book* for 2000, and therefore continue to have a presence in the settlement today. In a real sense these were core families, as interesting to historians as manorial landowners such as the Taylors of Middlewood Hall. And yet the social mix of much of the area had been dramatically transformed, for between the censuses of 1861 and 1881 the population of the parish (including Worsbrough chapelry) had almost doubled from 12,231 to 23,591. Wombwell's growth was spectacular, increasing from an already sizeable 3,738 to 8,451 in just twenty years. Change at Darfield was centred around Snape Hill and especially at Low Valley, where 50 per cent of all residents were born outside Yorkshire. A large number of migrant mining families had moved into the area from the West Midland counties of Shropshire, Staffordshire, Warwickshire and Worcestershire.

Darfield and Wombwell were given Urban District status in 1896 but it was Wombwell that really had the makings of a small town, with its busy High Street, markets and range services. It was so successful that the town centre was relieved by a by-pass in 1985 and underwent refurbishment in 2000.

There is much for us to celebrate and learn about the ancient parish of Darfield, but the recent opening of the Maurice Dobson Heritage Centre at Darfield and the excellent work already carried out by the Wombwell Heritage Society will ensure that the local history of the area will be made increasingly available for both present and future generations. It is hoped that this book will make a modest contribution to this process.

Many individuals, families and several organisations have been generous in loaning photographic material. I am very thankful for such help and kindness. Acknowledgement is at the end of each caption. Any unacknowledged captions relate to photographs owned or taken by myself. Thanks are also due to Simon Fletcher and his colleagues at Sutton Publishing for supporting the project and producing the book in such a professional manner.

Members of what appears to be a successful shooting club outside Hemingfield Working Men's Club, c. 1920. They are dressed for the occasion in very smart suits, white shirts and an assortment of fashionable headwear. The watch chains are also interesting accessories.

1

Knights, Farmers & Innkeepers

Detail of a monument in the south choir of All Saints' Church, Darfield, believed to represent the knight John Bosvile of New Hall who died in 1441. It was described as 'a faire monument in armour' by the antiquarian Roger Dodsworth, who visited the church in 1621. Over the centuries many individuals have been unable to resist carving their own initials into the soft alabaster stone, but interesting features of fashion and even facial appearance – such as the typical drooping moustache – remain. A word of warning, though, for any Bosvile descendants: by this time faces were usually purchased 'ready made', bearing little resemblance to the real person. *Tony Dodsworth*

PEDIGREE OF BOSVILE, OF NEWHALL IN DARFIELD.

ARMS. Argent, five fusils in fess gules, in chief three bears' heads sable.

CREST. An ox issuing from a holt of trees.

Sir John Bosvile, knight, 1252 and 1254.=Alice, dau. and heir of Hugh de Darfield.

John Bosvile.=Agnes.	Robert, living 1296; no issue.	Peter Bosvile, living 1296.	Beatrix de Furnival.	William, living 1296.	Matilda, m. sir Roger fitz Thomas, of Woodhall.	Catherine.

Sir James Bosvile, of Newhall, which he gave to Robert his cousin; no issue. | Adam Bosvile, lord of Ardsley, living 1302. | Matilda, who brought lands at Rykenildthorpe. | Robert Bosvile, constable of Pontefract 1333. | .... | Philip, living 1333. Edmund, living 1333. William. | Isabel. Elizabeth.

Thomas Bosvile, of Ardsley, 1344 and 1362.=Alice, dau. of John de Gunthwaite and Christiana his wife. | William 1347. | Sir Thomas Bosvile, living 1369.=.....

Roger Bosvile, living 1379.=Alice. | Thomas, from whom the Bosviles of Chevet. | Richard. | Margaret. | Anthony, living 1383.=.....

Thomas Bosvile, ret. 1388.=Margaret. | John Bosvile, of Ardsley.=Isabel, sister and coh. (with Agnes, w. of sir William Dronsfield, of West Bretton, knight. | | William Bosvile, of Newhall.=Joan. | Anthony.=.....

Mary, 1st w. dau. and coh. (with Margaret, w. of John Drax) of Thomas Barley and Isabel his wife, dau. and heir of John of the Woodhall. | John Bosvile, of Newhall, and Ardsley; d. Friday after Feast of the Assumption, 20 Henry 6, 1441.=Isabel, 2 w. dau. of Percival Cresacre, of Barnborough, executrix to her husband; m. 2 Henry Langton, esq. before 1448; both living 1460. After his death she took the veil of chastity, and was alive in 1480. | | Robert, mar. Emma, dau. and heir of John Vescy, of Coningsborough, from whom the Bosviles of that place, Warmsworth, Braithwell, and Ravenfield.

William Bosvile, of Ardsley and Newhall, son and heir 20 Henry VI.; living 1448.=Matilda, d. of John FitzWilliam, of Sprotborough, esq. | Richard Bosvile, settled by his parents at Gunthwaite in Peniston; from whom the Bosviles of that place. | Percival, 1472. | James, 1472. | John, 1472.=..... dau. of Rockley, of Rockley. | Elizabeth, married Thomas Anne.

Thomas Bosvile, of Ardsley and Newhall, son and heir.=Isabel, dau. of John Hastings, of Fenwick. | John, rector of Darfield. | John, a knight of Rhodes. | Richard. | James Bosvile,=..... son and heir.

John Bosvile, of Ardsley and Newhall.=Isabel, dau. of Nicholas Wortley of Wortley. | Hugh, rector of Darfield. | Richard. James. | Muriel, m. sir John Burton, of Kinsley. | Elizabeth, mar. John Keresforth. .... m. .... Dodworth.=..... m. Ralph de la Hagh. Isabel. | Alexander, living 1541.=Elizabeth, d. of Thomas Wheatley, of Woolley.

.... 1 w., d. of Henry Everingham, of Stainborough. | John Bosvile, of Ardsley and Newhall.=Elizabeth, d. of Ralph Reresby of Thribergh. | William Bosvile, of Wortley.=Jane, d. of Robert Rockley. | Miles. | John Bosvile, of Sandal, gent. 1546, Belhouse Grange, near Welbeck, co. Notts.=Jane, dau. of Charles Barnby, of Barnby.

Anne, 1 w. dau of sir Henry Sutton, of Averham, co. Notts. | Thomas Bosvile, of Ardsley and Newhall.=Elizabeth, dau. of Robert Nevile, of Ragnal, m. 2 Martin Anne. | Roger, 1 son, s. p. | Thomas, of Loske, co. Derby. | Emma, daughter of John Bromley, of co. Notts. | Christopher, son and heir, 1541; no issue. | Alexander.

Margaret, m. .. Fletcher. Barbara, m. John Mering. Elizabeth. | Lucy, m. .... Mangal. Ellen, m. .... Whichcote. | John, s. p. | Gervas Bosvile, of Newhall, esq. living there 1586.=Edith, dau. of Hugh Wyrral, of Loversal. | Eleanor. Ann. Douglasea.

Thomas Bosvile, of the New Hall, esq. son and heir, aged 23 1585; will dated 21 March 1637, proved 12 December 1639.=Ann, dau. and heir of Henry Drax, of Bugden, niece of Thomas Drax, of Woodhall. See p. 108. | Ann, m. Henry Savile, of Wakefield. | Jane, mar. William Broxholme, of Oleby, co. Linc. and had Elizabeth.[1] | Elizabeth, mar. Thomas Furnes, of Tickhill-Castle.

Hastings Bosvile, son and heir apparent, died young. | Francis. Gervas. Richard. } all died without issue. | John, d. without issue. | Mary. Elizabeth. | Ann, mar. Ralph Pollard. | Philip Rolston, of co. Notts. 1 husband.=Ellen.=Matthew Vescy, 2d husband.

William Taylor, of Nether Wood Hall.=Ellen, dau. and heir. | Bosvile Vescy, of Barley Hole.=Mary, dau. of Thomas Taylor. | Francis.

John.   William.   Ellen.   Mary.   Hannah.   Elizabeth.

[1] Broxholm married, secondly, Ann, daughter of William Marbury, by whom he had John and others. See Harl. MS. 5845.

Pedigree of the Bosvile family, taken from Joseph Hunter's *South Yorkshire*, 1828–31.

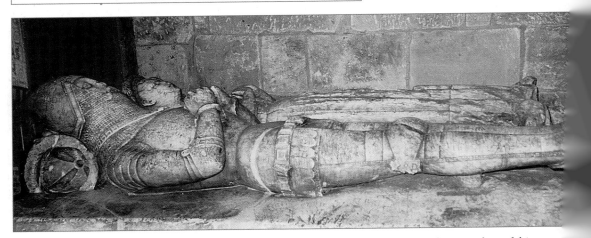

A knight and his lady in All Saints' Church, Darfield: effigies believed to be of John Bosvile and his seco[nd] Isabel, daughter of Percival Cresacre of Barnburgh. *Tony Dodsworth*

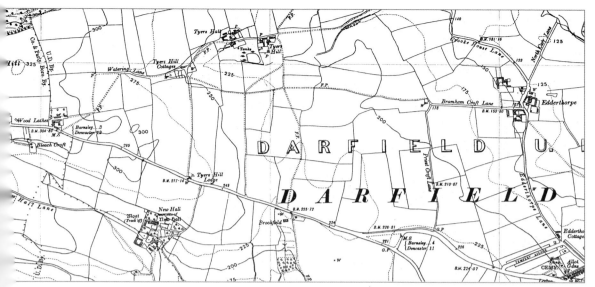

...ract from the 6 inch to 1 mile Ordnance Survey map of 1929/38 showing New Hall, home of the Bosviles, a ...dieval moated site in existence from at least the twelfth century.

...medieval hall known as New Hall was replaced by a substantial country residence during the eighteenth ...ry, with additions grafted on in the nineteenth and twentieth centuries. In 1946 the owner Ida Mai Wood ...ed its name to Cranford Hall, which it retains today.

A fascinating Edwardian glimpse of New Hall across what would then have been described as the farm pond, a water feature that may have been a remnant of a medieval moat. The stone archway is a surviving late-medieval gateway to the old hall and incorporates the arms of the Bosvile and Cresacre families. *Old Barnsley*

The 'farm pond' can be seen in the foreground of this photograph which I took on a visit to the site in 1974. The tenant farmer, a Scot, who lived in the cottage said he used to enjoy doing a bit of 'curling' when the pond froze over – and he showed me a granite curling stone which he kept on the pond wall. He also showed me the magnificent cruck timbers of the barn.

A general view, taken in 1974, showing the site of Tyers Hall (A) and Tyers Hill (B) farms. In the distance are the cooling tower of the power station at Grimethorpe. A series of ancient trackways connected medieval sites such as Wood Hall, New Hall, Tyers Hill, Crook House, Middlewood and the interesting Scandinavian settlement of Edderthorpe, which means 'Eadric's outlying farmstead'.

I first visited Tyers Hill in 1974 when the entire house was in need of considerable repair and conservation. Here we can see twin gables with partly blocked mullioned windows which appear to be of seventeenth-century date. The property, which then had few modern conveniences, had just been bought by Mr Graham, a Hoyland Common shopkeeper.

The north front of the house, facing the footpath, has interesting architectural features, including two-light mullioned windows, a massive door lintel and added chimneys suggestive of an earlier medieval building.

The south elevation of the house, seen here in October 1974, appears to have been given a stylish new front with tall three-light mullions, perhaps in the late eighteenth century. Tyers Hill and the nearby Tyers Hall farmhouses (associated with the Dickinson family) have subsequently been the subject of several prestigious awards in recognition of the wildlife and building conservation that has been carried out in an area erroneously thought of as 'industrially derelict'. *A.K. Clayton*

Land at Tyers Hill once belonged to the Priory of Newstead, and after the dissolution it was occupied by Sir John Byron (an ancestor of the famous poet), who sold Tyers Hill to Henry Reyney in 1569. Henry's son John, who was born at Smithley near Wombwell, was a member of the Company of Drapers in London. Not forgetting his roots, he left in his will £30 for 'a learned and religious preacher' at St Mary's, Worsbrough. The Reyneys were associated with Tyers Hill until the eighteenth century. Here we can seen an extract from the 1721 will of yeoman farmer John Broadhead of Tyers Hill. He had a large family but was sufficiently prosperous to bequeath 'four score pounds of lawfull money of Great Britain' to each of seven of his younger sons and a daughter. His eldest son William inherited the house and farm.
Borthwick Institute of Historical Research, University of York

Tyers Hall consists of a small group of south-facing eighteenth-century buildings standing only a few yards away from Tyers Hill. Three successively grander phases of building appear to have taken place. *A.K. Clayton*

The tall eastern wing of Tyers Hall has a pleasing Georgian façade and steeply pitched roof.

This former yeoman farmer's house, situated at Great Houghton, had a datestone of 1759 over a door lintel but the attractive two- and four-light mullioned windows are typical of local seventeenth-century houses. Unfortunately this interesting building has not survived, but was photographed by the author and Arthur Clayton in 1975.

Another interesting building at Great Houghton was the Old Crown Inn, seen here in about 1910. Perhaps licensee Henry Dey and his wife are among the people at the door of the inn. In 1917 William Ellis was the landlord and Mrs Ada Cook held the licence in 1936. The tall sash windows appear to have retained their original twelve-pane glazing. Also note the heavy stone-clad roof which would have had to be supported by very strong timbers. When first erected this building may have been a fashionable residence. *Old Barnsley*

The neighbouring Old Hall Inn was once one of the grandest small country mansions in the area. Dating from the sixteenth century, this fine gabled house with two cross-wings was the home of the nonconformist Rodes family, and became a shelter for Presbyterian dissent. *Old Barnsley*

In the 1880s Great Houghton Old Hall was described as 'disfigured and dilapidated' by local historian Joseph Wilkinson, and yet in this Edwardian photograph it looks in splendid condition, with the Rodes' coat of arms clearly visible over the central doorway. *Old Barnsley*

Despite political differences, Thomas Wentworth, who rose to become chief minister of King Charles I and was rewarded with the earldom of Strafford, may have been an occasional visitor to Great Houghton since his third wife Elizabeth was the sister of Sir Edward Rodes. After Thomas's execution in 1641 Elizabeth moved to Hooton Roberts, where she lived until her death in 1668.

a serious fire in 1960 Great Houghton Old Hall was demolished and replaced by the modern brick public e which has retained the Old Hall name.

In about 1650 Sir Edward Rodes built a private chapel in the grounds of the hall, which became a noted place for 'safe preaching' in very troubled times. Its first minister was Richard Taylor. He was succeeded by Jeremiah Milner and the last of the 'ejected clergy' to be appointed here was Nathanial Denton who died in 1720. The chapel had become 'united to the Church of England' by 1743, and remarkably it survives to the present day, a wonderful example of Puritan architecture.

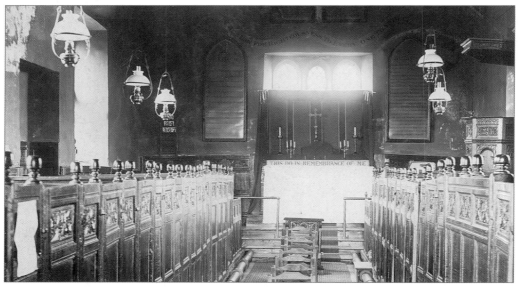

An interior view of the Great Houghton chapel, subsequently dedicated to St Michael and All Hallows, on a postcard sent by one of the congregation in 1913. Note the fine Jacobean pulpit and pews.

Wombwell Hall, seen here as it would have looked in the early nineteenth century, was one of the grandest small mansions in the area before its unfortunate demolition. Writing in the 1820s, the antiquarian Joseph Hunter described the house as 'still standing in the town street of Wombwell [but] divided into a number of sordid dwellings'. The hall was the seat of the Wombwell family from about the middle of the sixteenth century.

The old chapel at Great Houghton can be compared to the prefabricated 'tin tabernacle' erected in 1902 at Hough Lane, Wombwell. Known locally as the 'rubbing board' because of its corrugated walls and roof, it was bought second-hand for £70 and used as a church hall when the new red-brick Wesleyan Reform church was built in 1934. It was demolished on 15 March 1993. *Colin Massingham*

The ancient layout of the small village of Billingley can be seen in this modern aerial view. The main street, High Street (A), has a typical Anglo-Saxon parallel Back Lane (B), which encloses a number of old properties, including the Manor House and Grange and Rock House farms. The mid-eighteenth-century Billingley Hall (BH) stands out at the eastern edge of the enclosure, as does Beech House (F) which can be seen on cleared ground at the western edge of the village. Later, outlying farms such as New Grange and Holmes (west) and Hall Farm (east) are also visible.

The village is reached from the Barnsley–Doncaster road via Billingley Green Lane (D). At the Green Mr John Casson operated a carrier service before the First World War. A small number of properties can be seen on Flat Lane and Chapel Lane, the latter taking its name from the Methodist chapel (E) erected in 1818. Despite a small amount of modern development, Billingley retains a great deal of its rural character, with several old farm properties now converted for residential use.

BILLINGLEY

Private Resident
Stanley, Herbert, Billingley hall
Commercial
Appleyard, Ernest, farmer, Beech House farm
Ashwood, Fred, smallholder
Batley, Wm. Edw., farmer, Grange farm
Birkinshaw, Arnold, farmer
Casson, Godfrey, butcher
Cooke, Arthur, farmer, Rock House farm
Cooper, Thomas, wheelwright
Coulson, Wltr., farmer, Home farm
Cullingworth, Edwd., smallholder, Billingley grn
Firth, Jas., smallholder
Flintham, Jack, shopkeeper
Hellewell, Thos., butcher, Manor farm
Stanley, Herbert, farmer, Billingley Hall farm
Trown, Frances (Mrs.), farmer

This list of Billingley residents, taken from *Kelly's Directory* of 1936, demonstrates the almost unchanging rural character of the village, but there is no mention of the Three Horse Shoes, where William Goodworth was 'victualler' in 1822.

BILLINGLEY HALL, BACK LANE, BILLINGLEY

Outstanding 18th century Grade II listed detached residence enjoying a delightful situation on the fringe of this highly regarded village overlooking adjoining farmland. Billingley Hall is an outstanding example of 18th century architecture having been lovingly restored to the very highest of standards by the current owner. Providing generously proportioned and fastidiously maintained accommodation set on three floors, we feel this is a property which should not be overlooked by the discerning purchaser seeking a home of quality and character. Convenient for travel to Doncaster and Barnsley, A1 5.8 miles, Sheffield 21 miles, Leeds 23 1/2 miles via M1.

PRICE: £269,000

Billingley Hall, as can be seen in this modern advertisement, is a stylish eighteenth-century house, rightly listed for its architectural importance and recently restored by private owners to a very high standard. In 1984 the unrestored property was for sale at £30,000 and was described as 'of interest to Developers, DIY men and Entrepreneurs' but – in typical estate-agent speak – it also 'offered opportunities as a private home, super restaurant or rest home'. More recently, the Hall was advertised in the *Yorkshire Post* at £269,000.

Although somewhat faded, this is an evocative image of harvesting at Billingley in the 1930s. The girl on the horse is Mabel Crawford (née Coulson), still resident in the village. It was reproduced as a greetings card, sold on the behalf of Billingley Methodist church to commemorate the millennium. *Margaret Mann*

A wonderful view of the old Bridge Inn at Darfield when Doris Wheatcroft held the licence, 1920s. Another lady, Mrs Florence Elizabeth Noble, had the inn before the First World War (see p. 30). The much altered front of the building probably hid an interior containing late medieval features, since its strategic location on the Doncaster–Saltersbrook road made it a popular stopping place for private and commercial travellers from at least the sixteenth century. Stanley Dealey Wheatcroft, probably son of Doris Wheatcroft, had the inn in 1936, and in the years before its demolition in the early 1970s, Eric Hartsone was landlord. *Old Barnsley*

Beech House, Little Houghton (before restoration), photographed by Colin Massingham on 17 March 1982. Th
cottage had been empty for more than a dozen years when bought at auction by George and Diana Young, w
faced the daunting but interesting task of renovating the property. In the course of the work a huge oak 'marria
beam' was uncovered, bearing the initials 'H' and 'T', the date 17 March 1602 and the arms of the Tynd
family. This beam commemorated the marriage of Helen and Thomas Tyndale. Other discoveries included
curious bronze male figure buried in the wall of the house. Originally timber-framed with stone infill, the buildi
was plaster-rendered during restoration because of the weathered and porous nature of the stonework. The r
walls are of hand-made bricks. Beech House was occupied by a succession of tenant farmers and prior to its sal
the 1980s was owned by the National Coal Board. *Colin Massingham*

2

The Changing Way

Darfield Bridge toll-house stood on an open piece of land just off the Doncaster–Saltersbrook road and across from the River Dearne. As can be seen in this photograph, dating from 1982, it was a distinctive landmark. Unfortunately this historic building, such a telling reminder of the turnpike era, was demolished following an explosion at the property, which had been used as a roadside fish and chip shop and café. Oral testimony from an 82-year-old local man, recorded in the 1930s, suggests that a low wall stretched from the toll-house to the edge of the river on the opposite side of the road; the wall was broken by two gateways, the larger for wheeled traffic and the smaller for pedestrians. *Colin Massingham*

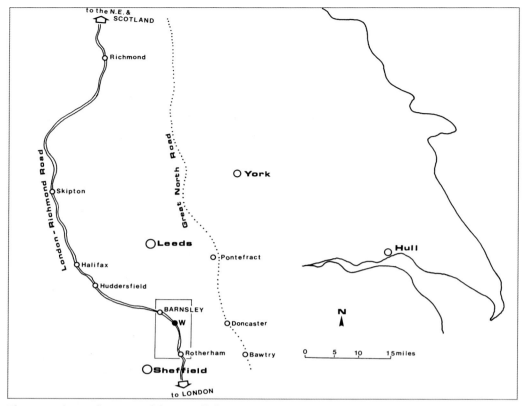

This map shows the route of the so-called London–Richmond road, the historic highway that ran down the eastern edge of the Pennines, roughly parallel with the Great North Road. As can be seen on the area marked by the rectangle, Wombwell, though far smaller in size than the market towns of Rotherham and Barnsley, was nevertheless also a convenient stopping place on this ancient route.

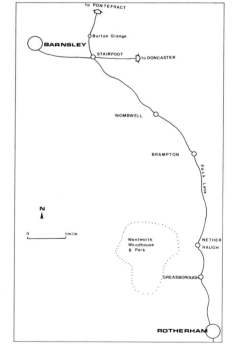

This inset from the larger map shows in more detail the Barnsley–Rotherham section of the London road. Only 5 miles from the market town of Barnsley and about a day's journey from Halifax, West Riding clothiers – who, as described by Defoe, 'go all over England with droves of packhorses' – found Wombwell a useful place to stop for refreshments or an overnight stay. At Stairfoot (which means 'stepped causeway') the London Road was crossed by another great packhorse trail – the ancient trans-Pennine 'saltersway'. Here, traffic could also proceed northwards via Burton Grange and on to Pontefract and York.

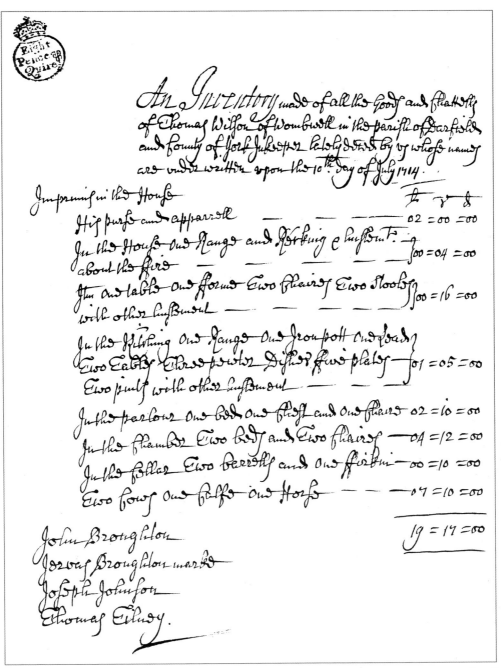

This is the probate inventory, a list of the goods and chattels, of Thomas Wilson, a Wombwell innkeeper who died in 1714. He wasn't a wealthy man and appears to have had a couple of beds, but we know from the War Office Returns in the Public Record Office that Wombwell had 24 guest beds and stabling for 20 horses in 1686 – by far the largest accommodation available in any nearby rural community (only 5 beds fewer than in the town of Huddersfield), emphasising its strategic location on the London road. *Borthwick Institute of Historical Research, University of York*

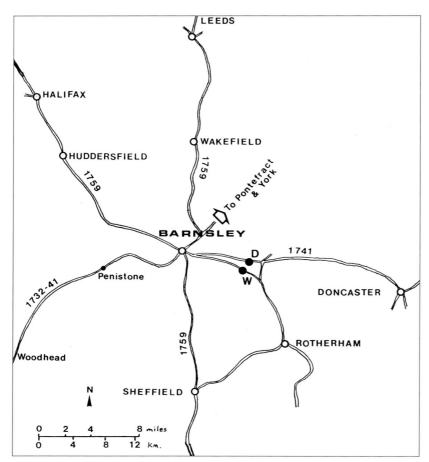

The continued importance of overland travel and its impact on small communities such as Wombwell and Darfield is well illustrated in this map of major highways in use in about 1760, when the coaching trade was developing fast and opportunistic landowners joined forces to invest in the new turnpike roads.

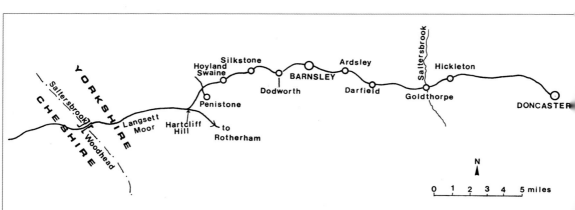

Ancient routeways such as the Doncaster–Saltersbrook road, as has already been noted, were of cru[...] importance to the economy of market towns such as Barnsley and smaller communities such as Darfield, though the moorland stretch over Woodhead from Cheshire was hazardous and often impassable in winte[...] 1723 it was said that the 'commodities to serve London and the Fleet came always through Barnsley, bein[...] more passable way than the moor towards Sheffield'.

Darfield=Bridge Bar.

TOLLS

TO BE TAKEN ON THE

Doncaster and Salter's Brook Turnpike Road,

Commencing 1st January, 1828.

		S.	D.
A Stage Coach, &c. carrying Passengers, &c. for Hire................each Time	—	6
Any other Coach, or a Chaise, Curricle, Gig, &c.	—	6
A Waggon, Cart, &c. with Wheels of 6 Inches	—	4½
Any other Waggon, Cart, &c. with Wheels of 4¼ Inches, and under 6........	—	6
Ditto...................................with Wheels under 4¼ Inches........................	—	9
Every Horse, Mule, or Ass...not drawing	—	1½
Every Ox, Cow, or Neat Cattle...	—	½
Every Calf, Sheep, Swine, or Lamb	—	¼

Every Horse or other Beast Drawing applies to the first five rows.

Post-Chaises to pay Toll on each *fresh* Hiring.

Manure and Lime *exempt* from Toll, when employed *only in Husbandry* for manuring and improving Lands; *provided* the same be conveyed and carried in Waggons, Carts, &c. with Wheels of six Inches, and used or laid on or in Lands in the Township or Townships through which the *Doncaster and Salter's Brook* Turnpike Road passes, and *bona fide* the Property of any Inhabitant or Occupier of such Lands.

Other Exemptions in cases of *Husbandry, &c.* as specified in the *Local* Act, (passed 26th May, 1826,) and the *General* Turnpike Acts.

GEO. KEIR,

CLERK TO THE TRUSTEES.

JOSHUA ROBERTS, Surveyor.

N.B. A Ticket from this Bar frees Harper Stables Bar.

PRINTED BY J. RAY, BOOKSELLER, STATIONER, AND HATTER, BARNSLEY.

Several examples of the tolls charged at Darfield Bridge survive, and this interesting example is from 1828, when fees ranged from a farthing to sixpence. *John Goodchild Collection*

In this fascinating Edwardian view of Darfield Bridge in the background, right of centre we can see the old single-storey toll-house, set back a little from the road. A carrier and horse and trap pause outside the Bridge Inn and a policeman stands with a smart-looking local. Beyond the tall wall is the River Dearne. On the far left at the junction with Pinfold Lane is a cottage that was the corner shop, and it is shown on p. 31, opposite. *Old Barnsley*

Frank Noble with his pony and trap outside the Bridge Inn, *c*. 1914. The man holding the pony is local blacksmith Tommy Bailey. Frank, whose mother Elizabeth Florence kept the inn, worked at Thomas Mackridge's ironmongery in Park Street, Wombwell. *Esther Johnson*

Mrs Ann Jackson, Miss Ann Jackson and George Jackson at the door of their Pinfold Lane corner shop, *c.* 1910. The Jacksons had taken the shop seven years earlier, moving there from Highstone Farm. The advertisement sign is for Hudson's soap and a bag of flour is displayed by the door but the jars of sweets in the window suggest that the little shop was popular with children, as can be confirmed by Esther Hannah Johnson (née Weigh) who was born there in 1915. *Esther Johnson.*

A wonderful and rare photograph showing a group of children informally assembled across Pinfold Lane, *c.* 1905. Several inhabitants are visible on the right, watching the photographer at work. Several of the lads are wearing clogs. *Esther Johnson*

Modern Darfield from the air. This oblique mid-1990s aerial view, taken from the south-west, shows us how modern, post-war housing has infilled the land between Barnsley Road (B) and Doncaster (Saltersbrook) Road (D). In the distance Middlewood Hall (M) has retained its parkland above a pronounced meander of the Dearne. *Wes Hobson*/Barnsley Chronicle

The old bridge at Darfield from the east bank of the River Dearne, *c.* 1910. The tall trees in the right foreground form part of the boundary of Middlewood Park. *Esther Johnson*

The Darfield Bridge area was often subject to flooding as can be seen by this photograph, believed to have been taken in the 1930s. An early 1900s flood was the subject of a poem by local stationmaster Will Shelton, which included evocative lines relating to the Jacksons at the corner shop and the great dam disaster at Bradfield in 1864: 'In the window of a little shop/A fine old lady stood/Her thoughts were forty years back/When she witnessed the Sheffield Flood.' *Colin Massingham*

This extract from the 1 inch to 1 mile Ordnance Survey map of 1908–13 shows how important the railways were in the economic and social development of the area, with the Midland line crossing the coalfield at Darfield and the Grand Central following the course of the Dearne & Dove Canal through Wombwell.

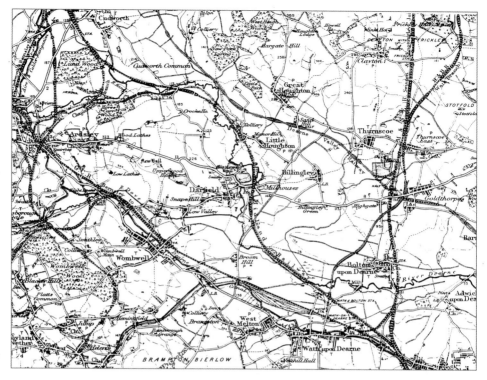

In 1911 a Sheffield–Wath goods train went out of control between Rockingham and Dovecliffe on the Great Central line, smashing into a shunting engine and wagon near Darfield Main Colliery. Despite the desperate efforts of the train driver, two men in the shunting engine were killed. Several postcards were produced to commemorate the disaster, and this example is by George Washington Irving of Barnsley.

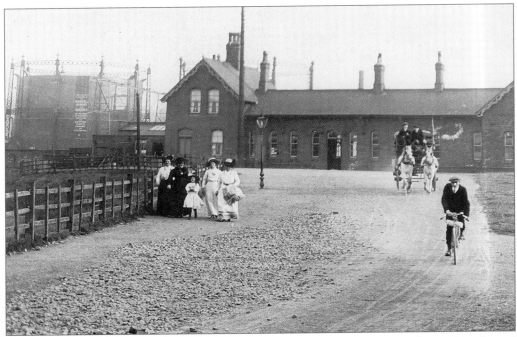

A two-horse carrier dashes from Wombwell station, preceded by a man riding a bicycle and watched by a group of women with a child, all wearing fashionable Edwardian clothes. *Old Barnsley*

A splendid early photograph of what was probably one of the first motor cars – a sporty two-seater – to be seen in Darfield, tastefully parked outside the Lodge at Middlewood, *c.* 1906. Mrs Gershom Noble (1855–1908) is being driven by Miss Ruth Noble. *Esther Johnson*

other superb photograph of an early motor car at Darfield, possibly in Garden Street. The driver is Mr Frank ble. *Esther Johnson*

A 3- or 4-ton lorry owned by builders F.B. Ward & Sons, in business in Barnsley Road, Wombwell, before the First World War, but described as of Littlefield Lane in the 1930s. Note the early telephone number. *Frank Burgin*

The stone bridge over the Dearne & Dove Canal at Bradbury Balk Lane (Mitchell's), Wombwell, fortuitously photographed by Colin Massingham on 30 June 1985. This fine and historic structure was demolished two months later. *Colin Massingham*

Another small but interesting canal bridge at Everill Gate Lane, Wombwell, photographed in July 1963, a few months before its demolition. *Colin Massingham*

Preparation work on the old Dearne & Dove Canal for the construction of the new Wombwell by-pass, June 1985. *Colin Massingham*

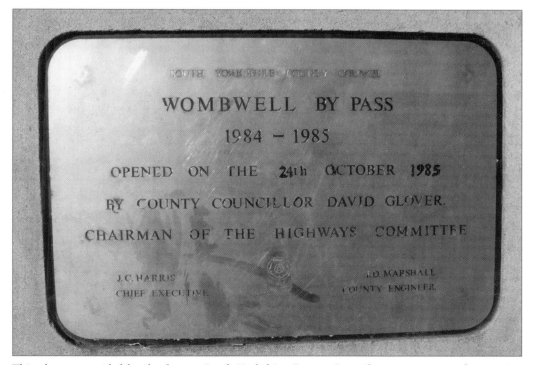

This plaque, provided by the former South Yorkshire County Council, commemorates the opening of Wombwell by-pass in 1985. *Colin Massingham*

The new Station Road roundabout at Wombwell by-pass, pictured in February 1991. *Colin Massingham*

Teenagers David Biffen (left) and Tom Gibson outside 58–60 Barnsley Road, Wombwell, setting off on a 'Tour of Britain' cycling holiday in 1964. The boy standing in front of Mrs Bessie Varney is Ian Perry, and looking on is Harry Varney. *David Biffen*

A tram makes its way along Wombwell High Street, on its way from Barnsley to Thurnscoe, *c.* 1930. The short-lived Dearne and District Light Railway closed on 30 September 1933 after less than ten years of operation, unable to compete with the fast-developing and more flexible omnibus services. *Old Barnsley*

A Greenhow & Sons bus in Wombwell market place, 1934. Greenhow's ran regular services for miners to and from Houghton Main. The 'day shift' bus set off at 5 a.m., arriving at the pit 20 minutes later, for a return fare of 5*d* per day or 2*s* 6*d* per week.

Tramlines are distinctive features in this early 1930s photograph of Barnsley Road. Also prominent is Charlesworth's corner Central Garage shop, the 'Authorised Ford Dealers'. *Old Barnsley*

A similar view of Barnsley Road, taken in 2001, makes an interesting comparison. Charlesworth's garage has become the Banana Hair Studio (with Tattoo and Piercing Studio above), some properties have gone and the curve of the street has been narrowed as part of the recent 'town centre' refurbishment scheme.

3

Middlewood &
Old Darfield

A carefully arranged group of fashionable ladies and gentlemen of Darfield, possibly a Bible class, *c.* 1900. The flamboyant hats of the ladies are typical of the period. The gentleman standing on the extreme left is probably Charles Howard Taylor. *Esther Johnson*

Middlewood Hall and its park from a 1905 postcard, which includes the line 'We play football on the lawn as you will see'. A medieval house existed at Middlewood but the present listed building, sympathetically converted into several separate residences in the 1980s, dates from the seventeenth century, but has substantial Georgian and later features. From Victorian times until the Second World War the house was synonymous with the Taylors, whose landed and business interests included mining and railways.

A formal studio portrait of Charles Howard Taylor, *c.* 1910. A very keen horseman, he enjoyed the usual country sports, being a leading member of the Badsworth Hunt, he carried on the family tradition of polo (a Yorkshire polo club was founded at Middlewood in 1890). He was remembered by Margaret Mann (née Longden) as 'an impeccable figure in riding habit on a sleek black mount'. At his funeral in the early 1920s the 'Squire's' coffin was carried from the hall to the church on a farm wagon on which 'a profusion of wreaths and floral tributes' were heaped. It was pulled by one of his magnificent chestnut horses.
Darfield Heritage Centre and Museum

Charles Howard Taylor (centre) with his gamekeeper Mr Kerl (to his right, wearing leggings), and a small shooting party somewhere on the Middlewood estate. *Esther Johnson*

Esther Harrison, seen here wearing her best black dress and lace hat, worked as a cook at Middlewood Hall, where her husband was farm bailiff. The Harrisons lived in Park Cottage. Margaret Mann, her great granddaughter, recalled the 'gentle rustling of her skirts as she moved . . . She wore a crisp cotton cap for dusting, . . . changed in the afternoons to a little lace-edged one . . . and for walking out to church on Sundays she [carried] a little black Dorothy bag lined with mauve silk that contained her glasses and prayer book'. *Margaret Mann*

Darfield Rectory, from a postcard sent in 1916. Walter Stonehouse, an exceptionally talented seventeenth-century rector, deserves wider recognition for his horticultural achievements, since he catalogued all the species of plants and trees in the rectory garden in 1631. His list of 866 plants, the earliest detailed record of a Yorkshire garden, included a fruit garden of plums, peaches, apricots and pomegranates. Arrested and imprisoned during the Civil War, there was little left of the garden when he returned three years later.

The Darfield Church Bible class must have been a very popular activity judging by this large group assembled on the rectory lawn in about 1910. *Margaret Mann*

A later Bible class, photographed outside ivy-clad Middlewood Hall, *c.* 1926. Note the unmistakable figure of Canon Albert Ernest Sorby MA, of Trinity Hall, Cambridge. Rector since 1892, he played an active part in church and village life until he died, while decorating his church, in 1934. The 1920s fashions provide us with an interesting contrast to those displayed in the previous photograph. *R.J. Short/Esther Johnson*

Church organists are often noted for their longevity of service. This is Gerald Strickland, pictured outside the the door of the vestry at All Saints' Church, *c.* 1925. Gerald was the church organist for about half a century. *Margaret Mann*

Mrs Lucy Bailey (left) and Margaret Mann outside Park Cottage, Middlewood, in 1978. Margaret's great-grandparents, the Harrisons, lived here. Mrs Bailey and her husband Tom, the village blacksmith, had succeeded them at the seventeenth-century estate cottage during the miners' strike of 1926, fifty-two years earlier. *Margaret Mann*

Lucy Bailey died in February 1998 at the remarkable age of 101, and was given a traditional horse-drawn funeral. For the last few years of her life she was a popular resident at Thornhill House. Barnsley Chronicle

terviewed Mrs Lucy Bailey at Middlewood Park in 1991 when she was 95 years old, and recorded some of her mories of Darfield on audio tape. The interior of her cottage had changed very little since the 1920s. She still d her Yorkshire range and 'modern' appliances such as a fridge and washing machine were only very recent itions, while oil lamps and candles had not long been abandoned in favour of electricity. She was born Lucy icock in a farm cottage at Edderthorpe in 1896 and was brought up by her grandparents, who took a farm at fton. Lucy recalled helping out with household chores as a young girl, making butter in the traditional way fetching beer from the cellar for the farm labourers at meal times. Labourers were still obtained at annual ute Fairs, hired by the farmers with a 'fastening penny'. Rising at 4 a.m. in summer, she had the regular tasks eding the chickens and milking. The family moved to nearby Cudworth and in 1922 Lucy married blacksmith Bailey in Felkirk Church. 'Squire' Taylor was pleased to accommodate the young couple at Park Cottage, re Tom would be on hand for his blacksmithing skills. He worked from the forge at Darfield Bridge. Lucy had y fond memories of the Taylor family and Darfield's long-term rector, Canon Sorby.

Iron railings enclose the grave of Darfield's most illustrious former inhabitant, the poet Ebenezer Elliott, who gained a national reputation in the 1830s via his *Corn Law Rhymes*, first printed in pamphlet form 'by order of the Sheffield Mechanics' Anti-Tax Society'. Elliott died at Hargate Hill Farm, Great Houghton, on 1 December 1849, aged 68. He was a virulent critic of the despised 'bread tax' and his verses in *The Village Patriarch* (1829) and *The People's Anthem* (1847) made a refreshing change from the establishment poets of the day. Regarded by some as a political propagandist, even a dangerous radical, he was in fact a passionate advocate for relieving the sufferings of ordinary people. Now an almost forgotten figure, Elliott deserves his rightful place among the great poets of the nineteenth century.

A 1930s view of Darfield Church and churchyard. In those days Elliott's grave was not so readily distinguishable since there were other plots enclosed by iron railings. During the Second World War all except Elliott's grave had their ironwork removed, apparently for recycling for munitions.

Darfield's magnificent medieval church, in the 1990s. The earliest part of the building appears to be the lower part of the tower where the rubble masonry is typical of a Norman structure, possibly replacing a pre-Conquest building.

An interesting view of the oil-lit interior of All Saints' Church from a picture postcard sent from Darfield in 1904. 'W. Stables' was a very able and popular local photographer with a shop on Snape Hill.

A fascinating view of Church Street and the old Cross Keys Inn, probably taken in the late 1930s. In the distance, at the corner with Vicar Lane, is Camplejohn's corner off-licence, now converted into the Maurice Dobson Museum and Heritage Centre. *Old Barnsley*

A wonderful early photograph of a very crowded Church Street, packed with a patriotic military parade on Sunday 17 July 1904, a few weeks after the successful defence of the British Mission in Tibet. It's likely that some of the men may have experienced active service in the recent Boer War. The sign of the Cross Keys and the ivy-clad vicarage can be seen on the right of the postcard. *Margaret Mann*

Church Street on a quieter day, with a pony and trap in the middle of the road and what appears to be an early motor car at the gates of the churchyard. Also note the large and typical Edwardian posters on the gable of the Cross Keys.

Many young Darfield men responded to Lord Kitchener's call to arms in the First World War and were killed in action, particularly on the Somme in 1916. This commemorative postcard was produced by the noted Barnsley photographer Warner Gothard for Darfield Conservative Club.

Although somewhat faded, this rare photograph from about 1904 shows a dozen men, a dog and, in the background, a young girl, standing outside Darfield Conservative Club, School Street. The tall bowler-hatted figure (Sydney Camplejohn?) stands out above the more typical flat caps. The man standing at the front (centre), hands in pockets, is George Jackson. *Esther Johnson*

The wartime programme of events started with a warship ball at the Council School, Snape Hill Road (9 p.m. to 2 a.m.), and later included a grand parade from Low Valley Recreation Ground to Foulstone Modern School, a cinema show at the Empire, a boxing exhibition, a grand football match (in the George Hotel grounds), a fun fair, one act plays (Darfield Dramatic Society) and a grand concert at the British Legion Club. All these events were held in order to raise £25,000: 'the cost of a motor torpedo boat'. *Colin Massingham*

An interesting Edwardian view of School Street. A woman looks in the window of the corner (butcher's?) shop next to the Reading Room and a small group consisting mainly of children watches the photographer undeterred by an approaching dog, setting up his equipment in Vicar Lane. *Old Barnsley*

A wonderful photograph of School Street by W. Stables, who no doubt encouraged children and adults to face the camera, including what appears to be a passing milk dray and occupants (Albert Avil?) of the barber's shop. In the distance is Isaac Jackson's shop. *Old Barnsley*

4

Snape Hill &
Low Valley

'Snapegate' is mentioned in the thirteenth century, probably in reference to a road passing through a boggy piece of land or poor pasture. The road that rose into Darfield from the valley of the Dove in the west developed into a residential and small retail centre during the late nineteenth and early twentieth centuries. A key family was the Hammertons, who between 1877 and 1894 submitted plans for the building of eighty-nine houses. Daniel Hammerton bought land near the top of the hill, owned by Trinity College, Cambridge, and erected there College House and College Terrace. Apart from building, the Hammertons also had a joiner's and house furnisher's shop selling, as we can see from this marvellous photograph, a considerable range of goods; they also functioned as funeral directors. The family was also active in local government, Ernest Hammerton, for example, serving as surveyor and sanitary inspector to Darfield UDC. Perhaps Holin Hammerton is the bowler-hatted man standing by the windsor chair. *Old Barnsley*

Snape Hill was a popular subject for picture postcards, mostly produced by local photographers. Here is an early example by W. Stables showing several shops on the upper part of the hill. One of them is the draper's shop of either William Henry Banks or John Lawson. Out of shot at the top, on the right side of the hill was an important commercial building: a branch of the Barnsley British Co-operative Store. *Old Barnsley*

This photograph, also by Stables, was taken a few years later from a similar position to the previous example, but is a better quality image. The solitary gas lamp appears to be a relatively new addition to the street. The trader's horse and cart adds interest to the scene, as do the men standing in the road who would have known the photographer well. *Old Barnsley*

Another interesting view of Snape Hill, showing some of the properties lower down the hill, near the junction with Havelock Street. A barber's pole is just discernible projecting from a house on the right. Arthur Taylor of Snape Hill is listed as having a hairdresser's shop in a 1917 directory. In 1936 there were two hairdressers listed: John Holden at no. 40, near the top of the hill and John Wright at no. 67. *Old Barnsley*

Two early motor cars can be seen in this photograph, taken in about 1920, allowing us a more distant glimpse up the hill. Also in shot is a small horse-drawn grocer's vehicle with a 'Brooke Bond Tea' logo on its rear. The building on the lower right (no. 91) is Darfield Working Men's Club, where Alfred Atkinson was secretary in 1917 and Tom Wilson in 1936. This card was published by Ernest Gardner, sub-postmaster at Darfield Bridge. The National Provincial Bank, shown on the right of the photograph, opened on Monday and Friday mornings, mainly catering for the needs of local shopkeepers. *Old Barnsley*

SNAPE HILL BUSINESSES in 1936

16, Long, Ada (Mrs), grocer
17, Lazenby, Robert William, motor cycle agent
19, Bibbing, Thomas Henry, shopkeeper
27, Burniss, James Robert, fried fish dealer
36, Lazenby, Robert William, wireless supplies dealer
37, Brown, Alfred, boot dealer
38, Neville, Leonard & Son Ltd, chemists & druggists & post office
40, Holden, John, hairdresser
54, Brown, Sarah (Miss), grocer
67, Wright, John, hairdresser
69, Webster, Frank Willis, grocer
72, Larvan, Patrick, wine & spirit merchant
74, Wyson, Elizabeth (Mrs), shopkeeper
78, Bissett, George, shopkeeper
80, White, Philip, butcher
88, White P. & L., butchers
90, Hardman, Thomas, hardware dealer
91, Darfield Working Men's Club
91a, Ellis, Reginald, cycle dealer
91b, Upton, Arthur, shopkeeper
92, Blaxland, Herbert, draper
94,Anderson, George, greengrocer
102, Hammerton, Holin, joiner
107, Fenn, Isiah, insurance agent
113, Banks, William Henry, draper
114, Coe, Wilfred, grocer

Also:
Barnsley British Cooperative Society, 18th & 63rd branches
Law, Harold, Victoria Inn
Marshall, Timothy, boot repairer
National Provincial Bank
Smith, Daniel, omnibus proprietor
Camplejohn Bros, motor bus proprietors

Snape Hill businesses extracted from *Kelly's Directory* for 1936. Properties with even numbers are on the left side of the road, looking up the hill.

Low Valley developed as a thriving mining settlement during the second half of the nineteenth century, but census information shows that most of its inhabitants were born outside Yorkshire, particularly in the West Midlands. Long-distance migration into the area must have created a distinctive community in contrast both to Darfield village itself and to Snape Hill. By the early 1900s there was a Mission Church and a chapel, and an enlarged infants' school for 110 children. There were at least seven general shops, a sub-post office, a pub (the George Hotel in Pitt Street) and working men's club, as well as a beer retailer, furniture dealer, tripe dresser, confectioner, butcher, painter, hairdresser and pawnbroker (Pantons, later Howells). This excellent photograph is one of series produced by Scrivens of Doncaster. *Old Barnsley*

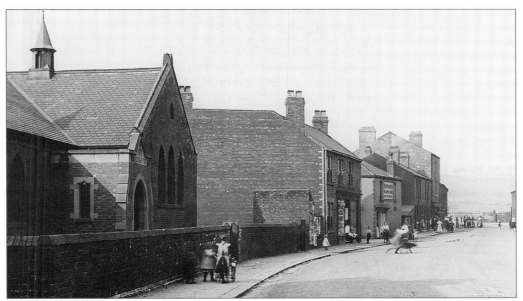

Another superb Scrivens photograph, *c.* 1920. Here can be seen part of the Wesleyan chapel on George Street, Low Valley and several shops, most notably Henry Hawson's 'building stores' – the rendered building with its advertising notice between the upper windows. *Old Barnsley*

In this 1920s Scrivens photograph, taken from the pronounced bend in the road at George Street, we have a good view of the cinema, school and church. *Old Barnsley*

A small group of people and a pony outside the solitary Bricklayers Arms (now the Drop Inn) at Low Valley in the late 1960s, at a time when many old terraced properties had already been cleared.

5

Wombwell

The Boer War memorial on the Station Road side of the former town hall at Wombwell is one of the best examples in South Yorkshire and deserves more than a passing glance.

The Urban District Council of Wombwell was one of several new Barnsley area authorities (including Darfield) that came into being following the Local Government Act of 1894. The building of the fine town hall, in 1897, was an understandable response of the fledgling council in dealing with its new responsibilities, and a useful way to celebrate the diamond jubilee of Queen Victoria. The resulting edifice was also an enormous symbol of civic recognition and pride in a burgeoning coal mining area that was continuing to attract new residents. The population, including those living in the outlying settlements of Lundhill, Hemingfield, Jump, Wombwell Main, New Wombwell and Wombwell Junction, described as 'hamlets' in early twentieth-century directories, was 13,252 in 1901 but by 1911 this figure had risen to 17,536, giving the central place the character and commercial facilities of a small town.

A modern view of the former Wombwell town hall shows that few changes have occurred to the exterior of the building, which continues to have a local administrative function as part of the Barnsley Metropolitan District Council.

(*Below*) Although somewhat weathered, the inscription on the foundation stone of Wombwell town hall is an interesting reminder of a ceremony carried out over a hundred years ago, in 1897, performed by Mrs Mitchell, the wife of one of the leading coal-mine owners of the Barnsley area, accompanied by Arthur Garland and John Robinson.

A busy High Street scene superbly captured by a local photographer, *c.* 1905. Horse cabs await customers outside the new town hall, another stops across the street while a paper boy and barrow boys pause in the middle of the road. Guests' distinctive pawnbroker's shop is partly in view on the left while the relatively new Charles Spedding's drapery emporium (now Dunston Brearley Travel),

with its 1895 datestone, has an imposing frontage at the junction with Station Road. Across from Spedding's is the Prince of Wales public house where Noah Nichols was landlord in 1912, and in the distance, abutting on to High Street from Marsh Street, is its competitor, Frank Reeson's Old Horse Shoe.

A splendid view of High Street from Park Street, taken by Scrivens, *c.* 1920s. We have a good view of John Guest & Sons pawnbrokers and jewellers shop (now the Churchill Hotel) which would have been particularly busy via its discrete Alma Street entrance on Fridays and Mondays. The white-painted cottage is a rare survivor of an earlier, probably eighteenth-century Wombwell. Miss Henrietta Wainwright kept the newsagent's shop, probably taking over from the Wroe family who were ironmongers. More recently it was 'Nugents' and now it's the 'Time Tunnel'. We also have a good view of the adjoining stone properties – the tall Bank Buildings and, nearest the camera, Woodbine Villas, which then had small front gardens. *Old Barnsley*

A modern (2001) view of the previous scene helps us appreciate how important early photographs are in our understanding of local history. A great deal of change has taken place but some continuity is also evident in the centre of Wombwell.

Park Street, Wombwell, 2001. On the left is the smart new Salvation Army building (succeeding the old 'barracks' on Station Road), next to St Michael and All Angels Catholic Church. On the right are Wombwell Conservative and Unionist Club (built in 1886) and the Wombwell Thespian Playhouse which occupies a former chapel of 1873.

A contrasting view of Park Street, looking towards Wath Road, by Scrivens, *c.* 1920. *Old Barnsley*

The drapery and tailoring departments of the Wombwell Barnsley British Co-operative Society branch on the corner of High Street and Marsh Street. The foundation stone of what was to become one of Wombwell's grandest commercial buildings was laid by Arthur John Wroe on 23 January 1902.

An interesting view of the new Co-operative branch and Central High Street when it was having one of i spring sales in the early 1900s. *Nora Turp*

The almost unrecognisable old Co-op building in 2001, now in use as an amusement arcade and gaming centre. I doubt if Mr Wroe and the founding fathers of Barnsley British Co-operative Society would have been amused at its modern transformation.

Arthur Wroe, the local Co-operative pioneer, laid the foundation stone of the new Wombwell drapery branch. As a boy he worked at the glass bottle works in Wombwell and then at Wombwell Main Colliery where he worked on the screens, in the lamp room and on the weigh-bridge, later becoming cashier in the general office. Such was the growing importance of Wombwell that there were also BBCS branches at Park Street, Barnsley Road and Station Road, while others served the mining communities at Wombwell Main, Jump and Hemingfield.

Another wonderfully detailed Scrivens photograph of High Street in the mid-1920s. These shops were located in a prime position at the centre of town. They are (nearest the camera) the newsagent's of Jabez Lodge & Sons, Harold Fisher's confectioner's shop, the Maypole Dairy

Company (one of the first 'chain stores') and David Neal's 'musical' store. The markets at Wombwell were established in the 1870s, and came under the control of Wombwell UDC. Saturday was market day. *Old Barnsley*

A new church in the Perpendicular style was built in Wombwell in 1896, replacing the medieval chapel of St Mary, which had itself been rebuilt in 1835. The western tower was completed in 1914, forming a baptistry, and in 1917 (during Canon William Henry Bateman's incumbency) there was said to be a capacity for 800 'sittings'. *Old Barnsley*

This modern (2001) photograph can be usefully compared with the previous example. Note the addition of the war memorial and the removal of the wrought-iron railings and gate, and the somewhat incongruous siting of the concrete lamp-post. We also have a more familiar view of the church with its western tower.

Advertisements taken from the front inside cover of Wombwell church magazine for November 1941.

A wartime wedding: Tommy Newsome and Betty Schofield at their marriage, St Mary's Church. *Nora Turp*

SOME WOMBWELL (HIGH STREET) BUSINESSES IN 1936

No	Business	No	Business
1	John Guest & Sons Ltd, pawnbrokers	2	Joseph William Kilner, butcher
3	Wilfred Wadsworth, baker	12	David Neal, music dealer
5	Fred Booker, baker	14	James Coombes Ltd, bootmakers
7	Joseph Mattocks, stationer	16	Maypole Dairy Co Ltd
9	Thomas Hinchliffe, confectioner	18	Harold Fisher, confectioner
11	Roy Butterfield, butcher	20	Sidney Bailey, butcher/Francis
13	Hardcastle Brook Ltd, wireless dealers		Elliott Warburton, confectioner
15	William Robinson, publican, Prince of Wales	22	Melias Ltd, grocers/Whites(Timothy)
17	Sterlings Ltd, bootmakers & dealers		& Taylors, chemists
21	Service Tailoring Ltd	30	Joseph Edward White, hairdresser
25	Thomas Coward, fishmonger	42	Edgar Wroe, ironmonger
27	Crossley & Cusworth, tobacconist	48	Charles Crofts, hairdresser
31	John Neville, boot & shoe dealer	50	Elizabeth Lockwood (Mrs), newsagent
35	Gallons Ltd, grocers	52	Edward Bramwell, circulating library
37	James Cernes, drug stores	52a	John William Cadman, wallpaper
39	Public Benefit Boot Co Ltd		dealer
41	Hunters The Teamen Ltd	54	Elizabeth Barker (Mrs), grocer
43	Webster, Brady & Sons, grocers	56	Midland Bank Ltd
47	Pearl Assurance Co Ltd	68	Ernest Tesh, outfitter
49	Alice Barker, greengrocer	70	Quick Press Ltd, cleaners & dyers
51	John Dook, butcher	98	Harry Charlesworth, hay & straw
53	Eli Blackham, jeweller	100	Harry Charlesworth, pork butcher
57	Norman Allott, accountant/ Alfred Robinson, grocer		
59	John Denton, china & glass dealer		
61	Oscar Ardron, draper		
63	British & Argentine Meat Co Ltd		
67	Harry Bellamy, pork butcher		
69	Ward's confectionery		
71	Exel cleaners & dyers		
73	Wilfred Barnes, boot & shoe repairer		
75	Myrtle Carr, fried fish dealer/ Ernest Denton, wireless dealer		
77	Meadow Dairy Co Ltd		
93	Charles Binns, baker		
95	J. Scarrott & Sons, hardware dealers		
105	John Lawson, fishmonger		
117	Lee Douglas, cycle agent & dealer		
125	Gertrude Davison (Mrs), confectioner		

Also:
Gas Showrooms
Barnsley British Co-operative Society
Burrows Motor Omnibuses

Source: *Kelly's West Riding Directory*

A list of Wombwell businesses located on High Street in 1936. Even numbers refer to properties on the right (hall) side of the road.

Church Street before the First World War when John Taylor held the licence of the Royal Oak Hotel. Frederick George Cusworth, listed in 1936, was probably the last landlord prior to the pub's demolition in about 1938. The boys in the street are 'hoss-mucking' – that is, collecting horse droppings for their dads' gardens or allotments. *Colin Massingham*

The present red-brick Royal Oak replaced its predecessor in the late 1930s and has characteristic Art Deco features, in particular the clock and doorway at the King's Road entrance.

Hough Lane was a popular subject for Edwardian photographers. The well-built stone-fronted houses with small front gardens were built between 1901 and 1905. Several here and higher up the hill have interesting name plaques of local or of more distant associations: Melton View, Rosemount, Fairfield Villas, St Austell, Dearne View and The Poplars. *Old Barnsley*

A modern photograph (2001) looking down Hough Lane and Church Street. Although now a hundred years old the terraced properties look in excellent condition. The swimming baths with their stone column entrance have filled the open space just visible on the previous photograph.

Potato and fruit merchant Mr T. Connelly appears to have parked his horse and cart outside the St George's Arms in this 1920s photograph by Scrivens. The wide road and its muddy surface shows that this was still the age of the horse. *Old Barnsley*

The exterior of the St George's Arms has changed little as can be seen in this recent photograph, but some distant buildings have gone and new properties have been erected next to the pub. The road surface has also changed!

This early postcard of Station Road was sent on 3 November 1908. The Wombwell Free Library, visible on the right of the photograph, was then only three years old. The foundation stone was laid on 25 June 1905 by the Revd G. Hatfield, Chairman of the Education Committee, the building being 'gifted' to the township by Andrew Carnegie. The gap between the properties on the left side of the road – where large posters advertise the attributes of products such as 'Shino', 'Brasso', 'Keatings Powder', 'Globe Teas' and a 'Drapery Sale' at Butterfields in Barnsley – was soon to be filled by a new Salvation Army barracks. *Frank Burgin*

Station Road in 2001, an interesting comparison to the scene of almost a hundred years earlier. As in other areas of Wombwell, the stone-fronted buildings have survived the years in remarkably good condition and, as we can see by the modern scaffolding, are worthy of further restoration. Companies such as Dunstan Brearley Travel, Pete's Shoe Repairs and Pizza Top are very different from the small businesses located here three or four generations ago: tailor Samuel Lofts, barber Bill Beardshall, fried fish dealer George Burgin and greengrocer Samuel Dook.

Linear residential development took place along Barnsley Road from about 1875 to 1910 in the form of smart terraces and small villas. This was a fashionable part of 'town'. Wall plaques in this area include the names 'Darley House 1895' (no. 62) and 'Primrose Villa 1900' (no. 54). The landmark spire is of the newly built Primitive Methodist Church (1902). This is the view from a postcard sent on 5 August 1919. *Frank Burgin*

This excellent photograph of Barnsley Road by Scrivens is undated, but was probably taken in the early 1920s, just before the Dearne Valley Light Railway tracks were laid. The horse-drawn carrier will soon be overtaken by an omnibus and we have a nice view of a small parade of shops (nos 2–8): especially Herbert Askew's (barber) and William Charlesworth's (furniture dealer) with his samples of wares displayed outside, attracting custom in the traditional manner. *Old Barnsley*

Many Wombwell people will remember using the sub-post office on Barnsley Road (Darley House, no. 62), next to R.J. Short's photographic business (no. 64, with its overhead door light). An unattended baby in a pram has been left outside the post office in this photograph of about 1965. *David Biffen*

Part of the former Barnsley Road post office can be seen on the extreme left of this modern (2001) photograph, facing the pedestrian crossing.

The small front gardens of properties on the east side of Barnsley Road were compensated for by long narrow rear gardens, as can be seen in this example behind no. 60, where baker Bill Downs lived in 1965. *David Biffen*

Harry Varney (1906–76) at his home at 58 Barnsley Road, *c.* 1965. Harry was a surface worker (driver) at Mitchell Main and Darfield Main collieries. *David Biffen*

A Wombwell UDC 'dustman' at work in the back yard of 22 Edward Street, photographed by Colin Massingham on 7 August 1964. Everyday scenes such as this were rarely recorded, so are always of interest. *Colin Massingham*

Slum properties in Marsh Street, *c.* 1932. Note the 'cobbled' (stone-setted) street, and strewn rubble from a demolished outbuilding. *Colin Massingham*

A long-lost reminder of country life: local historian Arthur Clayton, who celebrated his 100th birthday in June 2001, shows off the bee boles in a stone wall at Skiers Spring Farm, Hemingfield, in August 1971. They were built to contain bee hives or skeps. The wall was demolished shortly afterwards.

A reminder of street parties: a great deal of patriotism was expressed in mining communities for royal events such as coronations, weddings and jubilees. On the walls of terraced properties in Edward Street the words 'LONG LIVE THE KING/QUEEN' were still visible in the early 1970s.

This fine photograph by Scriven is labelled 'Darfield Road, Wombwell' but is of Station Lane, *c.* 1920. In the distance (no. 27) is Thomas Henry Jones's greengrocer's shop (with an unusual three-wheeled vehicle parked opposite), and at the end of the terrace (no. 17) is Glossop's, the wardrobe dealers who also operated the Imperial Steam Laundry. After Glossop's, at no. 15, is Tingle's grocer's shop and then the boot and shoe repair shop of John Richardson. The Fry's enamelled signs are interesting features. *Old Barnsley*

Another splendid and rare Scrivens photograph, this time showing Bradbury Road/Street, from a postcard sent from Wombwell to Monk Bretton in 1918. Also visible is the bridge over the Dearne & Dove Canal in the distance. Scrivens used to encourage people to come out into the street – it sold more postcards! Photographs of long-lost working-class housing and people are of immense value to anyone interested in family and local history.

6

Mines & Quarries

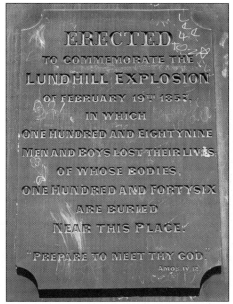

Taken from the obelisk in Darfield churchyard, this is the inscription on one of the saddest mining memorials in the Barnsley area. An explosion of firedamp blasted through the underground workings of the new Lundhill Colliery, near Wombwell, on a cold February day in 1857. The disaster was given front-page coverage in the prestigious *Illustrated London News*, a 'first' for a mining tragedy. The Kellett family lost five sons. Such events had a voyeuristic appeal, attracting 'coach loads of excursionists'. It was estimated that fifteen thousand people assembled at the pit head. Two years later Charles Dickens accompanied a party of literary men who toured the stricken pit. Paris was an option that they turned down.

Lundhill Row, a long terrace of nineteenth-century miners' houses, long demolished. The headgear of Cortonwood Colliery can be seen in the distance. Only the Lundhill Tavern remains; the adjacent area is almost unrecognisable today after extensive landscaping, including the provision of a golf course and a small lake set alongside a new dual-carriageway and the expanding Cortonwood retail park. *C. Lee*

Slightly detached from Lundhill Row, near the low white building in the foreground of the previous photograph, was the Lundhill Wesleyan Church. It is pictured here in October 1969, just before its demolition. *A.K. Clayton*

Lundhill Tavern, with its 'Barnsley Bitter' signs, October 1969. A.K. Clayton

all mining community known as Wombwell Main developed during the nineteenth century, serving the y of the same name. Nearby was a small railway station (see p. 99). This view, from the direction of well Wood, is taken from a postcard sent from Darfield in 1908.

The small row of terraced houses deliberately sited in Darfield Main Colliery yard was known locally by wonderful name of 'Donkey Kick-up Row'. This photograph was taken shortly before the houses were demolish in the 1930s. *R.J. Short*

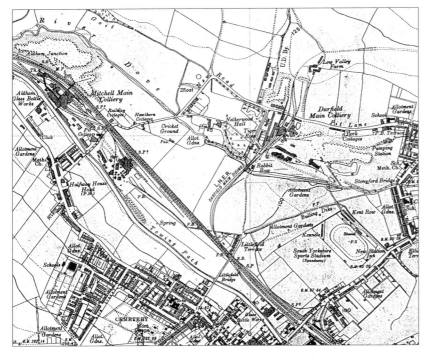

This extract from the Ordn Survey map of 1929/38 s the site of Darfield Main Colliery, which was linked sidings to the Great Centr Railway. It was only about a mile from its sister pit, Mitchell Main Colliery at Aldham.

DESTRUCTIVE FIRE AT THE DARFIELD MAIN COLLIERY, NEAR BARNSLEY.

At an early hour on Monday morning, the Darfield Main Colliery, near Wombwell, and about five miles from Barnsley, was the scene of a fire which at one time threatened to consume the whole of the material forming the surface plant. So serious a disaster to a colliery in this district has not been experienced since the well-known Oaks explosion. Happily, no lives have been lost, but the destruction of property will be very great indeed, seeing that there is an uncertainty connected with the opening out of the pit. In addition to the damages sustained by fire, the owners have lost forty-five horses and ponies which were in the pit at the time the fire broke out. The first alarm of fire was made known by the whistle or buzzer at the pit being sounded about eleven o'clock on Sunday night. This had the effect of causing the people in the district to hurry to the pit to see what was the matter, but long before they could reach the colliery their worst fears were strengthened by the flames rushing out of the pit mouth. In a short time they spread with great rapidity, and blazed into the air a distance of from 30 to 40 yards, illuminating the whole of the surrounding district. Those who saw the flames describe the scene as terrible, yet beautiful. The excitement in Barnsley and the district was heightened by the passing of the fire engines, with lighted torches, between one and half-past one o'clock in the morning. The colliery, it may be stated, has been at work for several years, and is one of the largest and most important collieries in the district, producing from 4,000 to 5,000 tons per week, and giving employment to from 400 to 500 men and boys. The disaster seems to be one of those events which no human foresight could prevent. Up to ten o'clock on Sunday evening, all was going on well, but it was then found that the cupola or up-cast shaft was drawing down, or, in other words, the air had become reversed. Mr. B. Wilson, the underground manager, was sent for, and he found that the metal tubbing or packing had given way, and the water was rushing down the shaft with fearful rapidity. This caused the air to become reversed, and drove the fire out of the grate, setting the slack and coals which lay about on fire. The furnacemen, whose name is Mitchell, made all haste to the pit bottom and escaped. The rapidity with which the fire travelled was very great, and having reached the pit bottom, it set fire to a number of loaded corves. As soon as the air was found to have become reversed, Mr. B. Wilson, his son, Jos. Elliott, and two fire triers named Ramsay and Scarson descended the drawing shaft, and found that the separation doors had been destroyed. Mr. Wilson, after setting two other pairs of doors open to turn the air off the fire, was obliged to come out. Two other men who were sent down to uncover the sump hole where the water lodges, in the hope of drawing water and pouring it down to reverse the air, had to be drawn out by the engine shaft, and narrowly escaped with their lives. The flames soon gained firm hold of the drawing shaft, which contained a large quantity of timber, and shot out of the pit mouth with fierce rapidity. The whole of the pit hill was covered with a wooden roof covered with slates, and on this being ignited the fire was communicated to almost all parts of the pit top. Several cabins and a small engine-house, together with most of the large and valuable screens, were destroyed or partly so. The massive head gear—one of the largest in the district—also caught fire, and some parts of it were greatly damaged; so much so, that it is believed it will have to be taken down. A number of loaded corves which were on the pit hill also caught fire, and their contents were converted into cinders. The pit hill yesterday presented a complete wreck; numbers of corves which had been burnt were only recognisable by their iron framework. The Barnsley Corporation fire-engines, which were sent for as soon as the fire was discovered, arrived as quickly as possible, and were got to work before two o'clock. Considering the extent of the fire, they did good service in keeping the flames from reaching the whole of the wooden tramways and the adjoining premises. Mr. Wilson, the underground viewer; Mr. F. N. Wardell, Her Majesty's Inspector of Mines; and Mr. Smith, the engineer of the colliery, were on the spot as early as possible, and remained throughout most of the day. The flames could be seen for a considerable distance, and this, combined with the fire engines travelling through the district with lighted torches, caused large numbers of persons to assemble throughout the night. Early in the morning, the drawing shaft was sealed at the top, and a large staff of workmen were got together and summoned to fill up the cupola shaft about thirty yards from the bottom. This work, it was expected, would be got through during the day. When the fire broke out, there were forty-five horses and ponies in the pit, which were valued at £1,500, all of which are, of course, lost. The disaster, in addition to causing 400 or 500 men and boys to be thrown out of employment, will entail great loss upon the owners, several of whom reside at or near Pontefract. It was only in February last that the coal caught fire and the pit was set down for some time. The present disaster is one of the most serious—loss of life excepted—that has occurred in the district. A large fire took place several years ago at the Wombwell Main Colliery, in the same locality, and more than a year elapsed before the pit could be again worked. Nothing like an approximate estimate of the damage can be made, but it must be considerable. There can be no doubt this accident will open people's eyes to the advantages which mechanical ventilation possesses over the furnace, for it is clear that had there been a fan the accident could not have occurred. It never can be safe in such a fiery seam as the Barnsley to have a great furnace roaring away in a pit where immense quantities of gas exist, the safety of many hundred lives merely depending upon a few wooden doors. Colliery managers, one and all, now confess that the furnace is not safe. Mechanical ventilators are being erected all over the country, to replace the furnace, which will soon be obsolete, from the sheer logic of facts.

---

xtract from *The Colliery Guardian* of 18 October 1872, in which a serious underground fire was reported.
ough there were no fatalities, the event resulted in a few months' hardship for the families of the several
red men and boys employed there before the pit was reopened. *A. Drury*

...t of a remarkable panoramic series of photographs taken from the disused Dearne & Dove Canal at Wombwell ...local man Colin Massingham in 1986. Darfield Main closed in 1989. *Colin Massingham*

site) Darfield Main not long before the pit buildings ...demolished in 1989. Developed by the Mitchell Main ...g Company, the colliery had functioned since 1916.

This wonderful photograph shows Jump Distress Committee during the 1926 miners' strike, when there w widespread hardship in the Barnsley area mining communities. The Salvation Army and impromptu groups s as this played a vital role in feeding children and poor families during the prolonged industrial dispute. Back (left to right): Fred Pantry, Herbert Broadbent, ? Whorton, ? Pettinger, Billy Hyde, John Lee, Wilf Boyd, Fr Evans, Louis Green, ? Hatton, Walter Evans and Noah Hill; middle row: ? Whorton, Bertha Pantry (née Bo Edna Lee (née Boyd), ? Swallow, Lilly Hyde (née Parr), -?-, Florrie Sanderson (née Allen), Mrs Hill, Mrs Jack Betty Evans, Mrs Sharp, Mrs Orwin, Annie Green (née Jolly); front row: -?-, Gertie Clifton, Edith Ev Mrs Beckett, Harry Haywood, Councillor Reg Preston, Maud Preston (née Boyd), Mr Bott, Mr Orwin, Mrs Mel -?-, Mrs Sidebottom and Mrs Carsley. *C. Lee*

Another superb social document showing ho difficult things were during the 1926 strik probably from the car of R.J. Short. Soup an bread are being serve miners' families at Darfield. Ingredients collected from local shopkeepers and by voluntary donation. A nominal charge w made of one penny f bowl of soup but the was always available to anyone turning u without any money.

Three Jump miners at 42 Church Street: Walter Lee (standing, with a child), John William Lee (sitting, left) and an unidentified man with a dog, *c*. 1929. *C. Lee*

Four miners in their Sunday best pose for a photographer in Wombwell Wood, *c.* 1910. *Old Barnsley*

The entrance (main haulage adit) to Dearne Valley Colliery, Little Houghton, 31 August 1963. Former miner Colin Massingham informed me that he was employed here from 1 May 1939 (aged 14) until 16 April 1967 (apart from a three-week spell at Darfield Main in 1946), when he transferred to a surface job at Houghton Main. On average, 200–40 tubs per hour were wound out of this 'day-hole' pit. Conveyor belts replaced tub haulage in 1968. The pit closed in 1991. *Colin Massingham*

An underground scene near the drift top at Dearne Valley Colliery. Forty full tubs have been made ready to leave for the surface, on Colin Massingham's last shift, 10 March 1967. Although Dearne Valley was regarded as a 'little pit', Colin remembers on many occasions having to walk underground for 75 minutes before reaching his place of work since the workings extended far out towards Clayton, Houghton Common and Grimethorpe. *Colin Massingham*

Colin Massingham was born in Darfield in 1925 and is shown here outside his Wombwell home in 2001. At the age of 60, Colin took voluntary redundancy after the miners' strike in 1985, having worked for more than forty-six years in coal mining. His last wage as an underground miner was £11 0s 2d in 1967, with a wife and two children to support. It is not surprising that miners became more militant for better pay and conditions during the 1970s. Colin told me that when he was a 'gummer', working on a coal cutting machine, he wore hob-nailed boots, stockings and short-legged shorts but nothing else apart from a helmet. Lighting was via a cumbersome 2-volt Ceag electric handlamp that weighed 7 lb.

Coal not Dole: the official picket, generally known as the 'Alamo', at Cortonwood Colliery, 25 January 1985. *T. Picken*

Dearne Valley Colliery Rescue Team, 1935. Left to right: T. Fisher, J. Lockwood, T. Marsh, F. Parkinson (instructor), M. Bray, J. Worthington (manager); front row: Fred Massingham (captain) and Jack Welford. *Colin Massingham*

rylin and Christine in the wages office at Houghton Main, 17 March 1982. *Colin Massingham*

nwell Main station and the 'Central Walk' leading towards Wombwell Wood, from a card posted in Wombwell
August 1905. *Nora Turp*

An early photograph showing the Quarry Hills area of Darfield. Sandstone was extracted by stone merchants Stephen Seal & Son, while George Atterbury & Company produced high-quality grindstones for the sharpening of scythes and other handtools from their Doncaster Road premises. *Old Barnsley*

Cox Bench House at Darfield Bridge, 7 February 1982. This was the former home of Stephen Seal and family.

7

Schooldays

David Biffen on his tricycle outside his home at
58 Barnsley Road, Wombwell, probably in coronation
year (1953). No micro-scooters in those days!

A very early school photograph dating from 1892, showing the boys of Standard 3 or 4 attending Jump Board (Council) School. Arms folded and stand/sit up straight . . . the lads look smartly attired, wearing long black woollen stockings and broad celluloid collars. William Melling is on the second row from the back, third from left. On the back row, third from left, is John Willie Lee, while on the next row down, on the extreme right, is Walter Blackburn. Fourth to the left of Walter is 'Cocky' Grayson of Hemingfield. The teacher, much liked by the boys, was Miss Lizzie Wharton. *C. Lee*

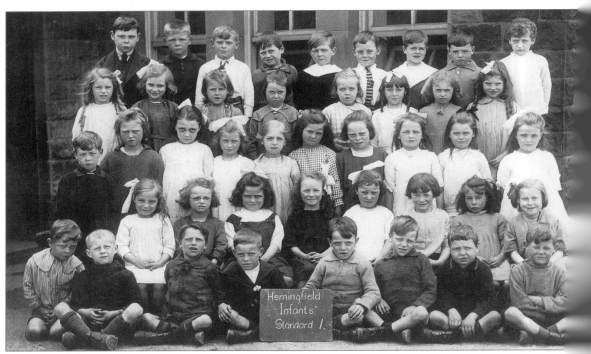

Standard 1 of Hemingfield Infants' School, photographed by Mr J. Blackburn of Wombwell, *c.* 1924. Back row (left to right): Alan Swift, Colin Bell, George Middleton, Sydney Askin, Ronnie Knowles, Albert Fowler, Norman H Joseph Cocking, Alan Morris; fourth row: Annie Frost, Elizabeth Wray, Lily Holmes, Hilda Heeson, Elsie Tomli Irene Middleton, Hilda Thickett, Grace Monaghan; third row: Harry Lisle, Connie Kaye, Emily Spencer, Gwene Carter, Sybil Ward, Eliza Watkin, Annie James, Eliza Rodgers, Phyllis Rance, Morva Bailey; second row: Stenton, Kathleen Skews, Rose Robinson, Mary Parkin, Ida Blackburn, Edna Moore, Isa Eyre, Emma Beevors row: Walter Stenton, Jack Rhodes, Jack Senior, Robert Allen, Albert Hellewell, Tom Lockwood, Harry Hunt, Briggs. Miss Cook was the class teacher and infants' headmistress.

Leslie and Colin Massingham on the front
doorstep of 22 Victoria Street, Darfield,
where Colin was born on 29 January
1925. Lesley died, aged 84, in 1997.

Class VI at Darfield Church of England Junior School, *c.* 1923. Esther Weigh (third row down, third
from right) stands out in her striped dress. The headmaster Mr Maud is on the far left. The school
was erected in 1840 and enlarged in 1900, for 286 children. *Esther Johnson*

The staff of Darfield Church School in the 1920s. Standing, left to right, are Mr ?, Mr Gibbs and Mr J.W. Hall and sitting are Miss ?, Miss Hall, Mr Maud (headmaster), Miss Darley and Miss Spencer. *Esther Johnson*

Many of the boys look happy in this formal school photograph taken at John Street School, Wombwell, *c.* 1929. *Nora Turp*

Some of the senior girls at John Street School, Wombwell, also have happy smiles in this photograph taken in about 1930. *D. and E. Biffen*

A more informal group of lads at Darfield Church School in 1933. Back row (left to right): Dennis Needham, Brian Keensmith, Herbert Steer, Charles Turton, Gordon Holbrook, Joseph Thorpe, Dennis Griffiths; middle row: Arnold Millard, Ronnie Manderson, Norman Furness, Walter Cherry, John Greaves, Rex Greenwood, Herbert Spencer, James Longden; front row: Jack Blount, Jack Galloway, Desmond Hibbert and Maurice Bardsley. *Colin Massingham*

A parade in honour of King George V's Silver Jubilee (1935), at the end of Cliff Road, Darfield, walking towards the old toll bridge.
Margaret Mann

Nora Turp and Brenda Fowler in patriotic mood at nearby Wombwell in the mid-1930s. *Nora Turp*

The (young) lady with the lamp: children from Wombwell's King's Road School took a great deal of care in their representation of 'Florence Nightingale' on a float that would have been appreciated by parents and spectators in a pageant held in about 1951. The school was built in 1905 as a 'mixed and infants'.

A wonderfully natural photograph from the camera of R.J. Short showing a group of children at a Wombwell gala in the 1950s. It also shows interesting fashion features. Note, for example, the lad in the checked coat and matching cap. Most of these children will now be in their mid-fifties! *R.J. Short*

Another superb early 1950s photograph by Short. On this occasion the lorry carries a load of children bent having a good time on Whit Monday, departing from Station Cottages (Dovecliffe Road). On the left stan Mrs Cooper and the children include Fowler, Sagar, Adams, Watson, Richardson and Meadows. *R.J. Short*

A coronation tea party in the garden of Mr and Mrs Pickles, Windmill Road, Wombwell. *D. and E. Biffen*

Class of 1963 (5BT), Wombwell High School. Back row (left to right): Mick Noble, Frank Hartley, John Crossley, Keith Binney, Stan Casson, John Mellard, Clive Baker; middle row: Brian Howarth, ? Parkinson, Tom Gibson, ? Stenton, Lewis Norris, David Biffen, ? Lunn, Dave Greenfield, Philip Robinson, Ken Dransfield; front row: Steve Creswell, Graham James, John Thorpe, Mr Ripley, Victor Betts, David Sykes, Graham Bell. *D. Biffen*

A group of sixth form pupils enjoy a social event at Wombwell High School in 1964. *D. Biffen*

Staff at Shroggs' Head Infants' (Darfield), enjoy a bottle of school milk in June 1957. Left to right: -?-, Mrs Dransfield, Mrs Hotchkiss (standing), Mrs Bladen, Miss Jackson, Miss Turton (standing), -?-. *Esther Johnson*

Some members of Barnsley Road Methodist Church Youth Club, *c.* 1963/4. The lad with the Buddy Holly glasses acting as DJ is Albert Young and the tall youth at the back is John Crowther, with Ian Cartwright on his left. Chris Fell is at the front. *D. Biffen*

8

People, Places & Pastimes

Wombwell women make a start preparing vegetables for the huge 'Collier's Pie', the main attraction of the Hospital Carnival in June 1938. The principal ingredients consisted of 1,000 lb of meat, 224 lb of flour, 5 bags of potatoes, 100 lb of lard and 16 lb of baking powder. The giant pie weighed a ton and was cooked in the carnival field, Station Road, in a dish made by the Wombwell Foundry & Engineering Company. Some 2,676 portions at 1s 6d were sold on souvenir plates (now collectors' items) provided by Wombwell UDC, bought from Edgar S. Wroe & Son at a cost of £75 5s 3d. The three-day event included the crowning of the Carnival Queen, Florence Frost, a well-known local musician. *Nora Turp/Blackburns*

This fine professional photograph by Joseph Alexander of Barnsley shows the Shepherd family outside their home at Milton Street, Shipcroft, Wombwell, *c.* 1900. The group consisted of Jack and Elizabeth ('Polly') Shepherd (née Hetherington), and, their children (left to right) 'Ginnie', Emily, Edith and Nellie – with baby Harold on her mum's knee. At this time photographers, despite their incredibly bulky equipment, were prepared to accept 'on location' commissions, though getting the right backdrop was never easy – note the crudely placed rug. *Nora Turp*

Fred Massingham, Divisional Superintendent, St John's Ambulance Brigade, at Snape Hill, Darfield, in Silver Jubilee year (1935). *Colin Massingham*

her high-quality family photograph by an unknown professional photographer, this shows Mr Gershom and Florence Noble and their five children, Walter, Lottie, Harry (left to right, standing), Frank and Ruth g), outside their home at Darfield Bridge, *c.* 1895. They are well prepared for the occasion, judging by their appearance. The sailor suits worn by the boys are typical of the late Victorian/early Edwardian period. *Johnson*

Mr Ken Blackburn of Wombwell in RAF uniform in the 1940s. Blackburns were noted professional photographers. *D. and E. Biffen*

Photographs of wedding groups can be fascinating social documents, as well as interesting in the history of fashion. This party relates to the wedding of Kenneth Blackburn and Edna Newsome in 1934. White weddings had become traditional by the late 1930s. The bride is wearing a stylish 'Princess Marina' diadem-shaped tiara and her young bridesmaids wear pretty long dresses of tiered material with a frilled neckline. The small page boy appears a little ill at ease in his outfit. The older bridesmaids/attendants are wearing long floral dresses and rows of frills towards the hem. Notice also their fashionable brimmed hats, not hiding their faces, and their stylish gloves. The groom's father Joe Blackburn is on the extreme left (standing) and his wife is seated, wearing a dark floral hat. Thomas Newsome, the bride's father, was Chairman of Wombwell UDC in the coronation year of 1953. The photograph was taken in the garden of Snowden Terrace after the wedding in the Barnsley Road Methodist Church, Wombwell. *D. and E. Biffen/Blackburn/Newsome family*

An interesting photograph of a Wombwell wedding group dating from the late 1920s or early 1930s. It relates to the wedding of 'Ginnie' Shepherd, née Swift. The bride has chosen to wear a colourful floral 'garden party' dress. *Nora Turp*

Wedding photograph showing Elizabeth Cherry and Hedley Longden, Darfield Parish Church, 11 September 1920. Note the bride's long veil and very stylish calf-length dress. *Margaret Mann*

A tea party (possibly in celebration of an engagement) in the Sunday School Room of Barnsley Road Methodist Church, *c.* 1959. The party includes Revd Fell. *D. and E. Biffen*

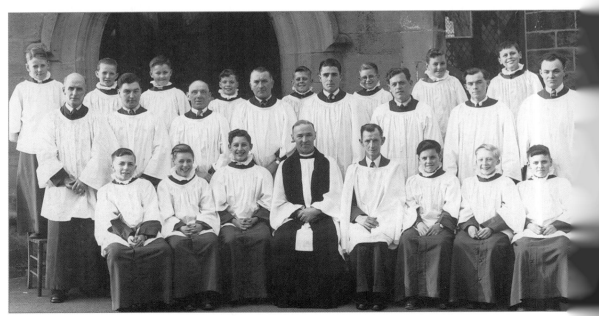

The Revd Casson and Darfield Church choir, *c.* 1954. Martyn Johnson (or 'metal detecting Martyn'), a re contributor to BBC Radio Sheffield's *Tony Capstick Show*, is on the back row, extreme right. *Esther Johnson*

Joe Travers, who was generally known by the nickname 'Soft Joe Jump', a local character who may well be remembered by older residents and former residents of Jump village. *C. Lee*

An anniversary gathering of children at Hough Lane Methodist Church, *c.* 1950. Mrs Cooper is seated at the front, on the extreme left of the photograph, and next to her is Mrs Newsome; while Mrs Hannigan, her daughter, is at the front, right (wearing spectacles). The lady in the floral dress and glasses is Enid, the Sunday school teacher. *R.J. Short/D. and E. Biffen*

The Maurice Dobson Museum and Heritage Centre, 2 Vicar Road, Darfield, officially opened to the public at Eas 2001 and offers visitors an opportunity to view and discover many items relating to the history of Darfield a the surrounding area. The Georgian building has been restored to an exceptionally high standard by the Y architects Martin Stancliffe (executed by Irwins Ltd) after many years of hard work by the Darfield Amer Society, with the help of funding from a number of individuals and trusts; substantial contributions were a made from the Heritage Lottery Fund and the European Community's RECHAR scheme which suppc regeneration in former coal mining areas. Facilities at the centre include a shop selling the work of lc craftspeople, books, souvenirs and so on; a room displaying antiques collected by the former owner and a c also used as a meeting and display area for local artists; and two superb upstairs display rooms. The museu open on Saturdays (10 a.m. – 2 p.m.); Sundays (2 p.m. – 5 p.m.) and Wednesdays (1 p.m. – 4 p.m). The musc is a tremendous educational resource for both children and adults, and arrangements can be made for group v when the building would otherwise be closed: contact Geoffrey Hutchinson 01226 753440 or v www.Darfield.co.uk

This photograph, dating from 1992, gives us some idea what the exterior of 2 Vicar Road looked like prior to its recent restoration. For many years it functioned as a corner shop and off licence (Camplejohns), and in 1956 was purchased by Maurice Dobson who continued its commercial usage, with his friend Michael Halliday. A keen collector and dealer of antiques, Maurice, who died in 1990, willed the property and its contents into what is now called 'The Maurice Dobson Trust' for the use of Darfield Amenity Society. *Gerald Hutchinson*

Monday, September 7th—   2 Days
George MONTGOMERY, Helena CARTER in
THE PATHFINDER Ⓤ
(Technicolor)

Wednesday, September 9th—   2 Days
BONAR COLLEANO, MARY CASTLE in
EIGHT IRON MEN Ⓐ

Friday, September 11th—   2 Days
RANDOLPH SCOTT, DONNA REED in
HANGMAN'S KNOT
Ⓤ (All Colour)

Monday, September 14th—   2 Days
SPENCER TRACY, GENE TIERNEY in
Plymouth Adventure Ⓤ

Wednesday, September 16th—   2 Days
GLENN FORD, ANN VERNON in
TIME BOMB Ⓤ

Friday, September 18th—   2 Days
STEWART GRANGER, DEBORAH KERR in
PRISONER OF ZENDA
Ⓤ (All Colour)

Monday, September 21st—   2 Days
CLAUDE RAINS, MARTA TOREN in
**The Man Who Watched
the Trains Go By** Ⓐ

Wednesday, September 23rd—   2 Days
Valerie HOBSON, Edward UNDERDOWN in
THE VOICE OF MERRILL Ⓐ

Friday, September 25th—   2 Days
EDMUND KNIGHT, MAUDIE EDWARDS in
GIRDLE OF GOLD Ⓤ

Monday, September 28th—   2 Days
ROBERT TAYLOR, ELEANOR PARKER in
ABOVE AND BEYOND Ⓐ

Wednesday, September 30th—   2 Days
RED SKELTON, JANE GREER in
THE CLOWN Ⓐ

Friday, October 2nd—   2 Days
MARK STEVENS, JEAN KENT in
THE LOST HOURS Ⓤ

Cinema programme (once nightly at 6.30 p.m. but two shows on Saturdays, 6.00 p.m. and 8.30 p.m.) for the Darfield Empire on September 1953, when the proprietor was R.T. Redmayne. The prices: balcony 1s 6d; and 'area' 10d and 6d.

Wombwell Colliers Speedway Team, 1947. The Station Road track was opened by Joe Baksi, world heavyweight boxing champion, on 9 May 1947 but closed in September 1948. *Colin Massingham*

Cortonwood Wesley Guild Football Club, season 1910–11. They won the Wombwell Walton Charity Cup and 'B' Division of the Barnsley and District Sunday School League. *Colin Massingham*

A group of girls, probably at Wombwell Baths, in the 1960s. *D. Biffen*

The well-prepared float for the Wombwell Hospital Carnival Queen, in the mid-1930s. The organising party/committee are (left to right): Edna Blackburn (née Newsome) with baby Wendy; Mrs Emily Schofield, Mrs Webb, Mr Webb, Mrs Clara (?) Newsome and Vera Schofield. The little girl with the flag is Nora Schofield. *Nora Turp*

The Guide Post Inn Women's Football Team, *c.* 1948. Back row (left to right): Dorothy Sanderson, Pat Bedford, Phyllis Duke, Nora Auckland, Ethel Briggs, Lily Calvert; front row: Mrs Harvey, Elsie Goulding, Mrs Siddens, Mrs Northburn, Kathleen Scott.

The first omnibus, a 14-seater, owned by Camplejohns of Wombwell – it must have caused a sensati when it first appeared on local roads. It was used for picnic and seaside trips, which became the highlight life in the mining community. The firm was founded in 1905 by Walter and Thomas Septimus Camplejoh 'Camps' continued to operate until 1960 when Yorkshire Traction took them over.

Members of Jump Operatic Society appear to be taking part in a scene from a Georgian production, probably dating from before the First World War. They were succeeded by the Wombwell Operatic Society in the 1930s. *C. Lee*

This poster may bring back memories for those who participated in or attended a production of *The King and I* at Wombwell High School in the early 1970s. *Nora Turp*

WOMBWELL HIGH SCHOOL
OPERATIC AND DRAMATIC SOCIETY

'The King and I'

(Rodgers and Hammerstein)

High School
Monday Nov. 30
to Saturday Dec. 5
7-15

Adults 25p (5/-)
Children 15p (3/-)
OAPs 15p (3/-)
All seats 25p Friday – Saturday

Book at the School or by post through
R. D. CARR, High School, Roebuck Street

Thornsby, Printer, Wombwell. Phone : 2257

Many Wombwell people will remember the Wombwell Empire Theatre and Cinema on Cheapside (Park Street). The building was officially opened on 12 May 1910 as a roller-skating rink and cinema. *Colin Massingham*

The demolition of Wombwell Empire (and the Empire hairdressing salon), 8 March 1965. *Colin Massingham*

...mbwell Working Men's Club and Institute's 'New Wing' in 1910. The club was founded in 1899. *Frank Burgin*

R.J. 'Joe' Short (1903–81) worked at Darfield Main and Houghton collieries from the age of 13 and was a very able amateur photographer. Some of the superb photographs he took during the inter-war period are now of considerable interest and importance as social and historic documents. He 'turned professional' in about 1950, working from studios in Station Road and Barnsley Road. I acknowledged Joe's tremendous photographic contribution when compiling a paper on local pioneering photographers published a few years ago by the Royal Photographic Society. An exhibition celebrating Joe's work, organised by Wombwell Heritage Society at St Mary's Church in June 2000, was an enormous success. This excellent portrait is by Roy Portman of Barnsley Photographic Society. *Roy Portman*

David Biffen, surrounded by a group of young admirers while on photographic duty at a wedding at Darfield Church in 1965. *D. Biffen*

A Sunday tea at 58 Barnsley Road, Wombwell, at Christmas, *c.* 1965. Joe Short is on the right, wearing a pullover. Others in the photograph include David Short (Joe's son), Clare Short, and Perry and Roy Carron. *D. Biffen*

t of a Whitsun gathering of local churches, assembled with their banners in the fairground, Wombwell, with
g's Road School in the background, *c.* 1965.

The start of the men's 10,000-metre cross-country race held at Brampton Ings, 14 October 1979.
As a Barnsley Road Runner, I finished well down the field in 44th position, but remember an
unaccustomed sudden burst of speed when encountering galloping stray horses on one of the laps.
The meeting was attended by nearly three hundred athletes from ages 8 to adult, as part of the
South Yorkshire Cross-Country League.

A group of girl guides from Barnsley Road Methodist Church enjoying a camp at Sewerby Park, near Bridlington, *c.* 1950. *H. Hoggarth*

Some of the staff at Darfield (Health) Clinic party, Christmas 1953. Far row (left to right): District Nurse Simpson, Mrs Shaw, the Revd F.A. Casson, Dr J.W. Whitworth, the Revd S. Milner; near row: -?-, Clinic Nurse Lodge, Dr Banner, Mrs Milner, -?-, -?-. *Geoff Harrison*